FOR
Cluck's
Sake!

FOR Cluck's Sake!

An "Egg"cellent Collection of
Chicken Lore, Chicken Facts,
Chicken Trivia & Chicken Love

STACIA TOLMAN

Andrews McMeel
PUBLISHING®

INTRODUCTION

This book—the facts and history and certainly the takeaway bits of wisdom—has been inspired by the many chickens I've known. Over the years, my backyard chicken flock has always been small enough that I get to know my chickens very well. Not all of them have had names, but each one, to a chicken, has had personality.

One of my favorite chickens was a Blue Andalusian that I raised from a day-old chick. This chicken had a wild spirit and would roost on the roof of my house, but in the morning, she would perch comfortably on my shoulder. Another favorite was our Belgian Bearded d'Uccle named Louie, named after the five-foot four-inch French king Louis XIV, because he was so tiny and regal. Louie would sidle up to our two very large Brahma hens named Selma and Patty (named after Homer Simpson's sisters-in-law) and perform his amorous rooster jig for them, but they would just kick poor Louie aside in irritation. Louie loved the banjo and would dance and cluck in time whenever my son would play the theme song from *Deliverance*.

My current group consists of four Ameraucanas, which lay eggs that are a lovely porch-ceiling blue, and a pair of Blue Laced Red Wyandottes. Recently, they have taken to roosting in the rafters of their henhouse. When I go to shut them in, I can't resist reaching up and giving their fluffy undercarriage a good-night pat. This gesture is a little beneath their dignity, and they murmur a soft complaining sound, which is kind of reassuring somehow.

The more I learn about and from chickens, the more interesting they get. I hope it is the same for you too.

Stacia Tolman

Wyandotte

Wyandottes originated in New York State and were named after a Native American tribe. The original Wyandotte chicken was the silver-laced variety, with white feathers with black edges, an effect called lacing. Since then, breeders have developed golden-laced, blue-laced red, chocolate partridge, lavender, silver-penciled, and numerous other showy varieties. Although it was considered endangered, The Livestock Conservancy recently "graduated" the breed from the endangered list, due to its popularity with backyard chicken owners.

Standard weights: Cock: 8.5 lbs.; Hen: 6.5 lbs.

> "If I didn't start painting, I would have raised chickens." —Grandma Moses

Chickens can see color better than humans do. While we have three cones to help us differentiate red, green, and blue, chickens have those three and a fourth that sees violet and ultraviolet light. A fifth cone in a chicken's eye assists with detecting motion.

〜〜〜

Although hen's teeth are "as rare as hen's teeth," they do exist. A recessive gene for hen's teeth was discovered in a lab. The gene for hen's teeth is lethal, so a chick expressing that gene will die in the egg.

〜〜〜

Chicken scratch embroidery is a name for an Amish style of embroidery in which Amish women stitch a design onto inexpensive fabric like gingham as a way of creating an attractive lacelike pattern. Aprons and curtains were typically dressed up like this during the 1930s, which gave it its other name of "depression lace."

Chickens have an impressive memory. They can differentiate and remember as many as one hundred faces (within and outside of their own species). This ability is important in pack species, where pecking order rules.

"The longer I live, the more beautiful ~~life~~ a chicken becomes."
—Frank Lloyd Wright

Chickens lay different colors of eggs. Biliverdin, a pigment produced in the shell gland of a chicken, makes for a blue egg; protoporphyrin, a different pigment produced in the shell gland, makes a brown egg. Pink eggs are the result of very small amounts of the brown egg pigment, and green eggs have equal amounts of blue and brown pigments.

NUGGET OF CHICKEN WISDOM:

There is joy in being well rested. Try going to bed when the sun goes down.

Chickens generally go to their roost thirty to sixty minutes before twilight. Earlier on an overcast day, later on a clear one. They come down from their roost about a half hour before daybreak.

Chicken Tetrazzini

Diced chicken and mushrooms in butter, parmesan, and cream sauce spiked with sherry and often baked as a casserole with noodles. The dish is named for Italian soprano Luisa Tetrazzini.

In the ninth century, Pope Nicholas I declared the rooster as the symbol for Christianity and had it placed on steeples either on top of the cross or instead of the cross, as a reminder of the fear of the apostle Peter, who was to become the first pope of Christendom and who denied Christ three times before the cock crowed.

Brahma

Sometimes called the King of All Poultry, the Brahma chicken is most known for its great size and strength. This chicken contributed to what is known as "Hen Fever," the American and British infatuation with fancy poultry breeds that hit in the mid-nineteenth century. For about seventy years, the Brahma was the most popular meat chicken in the United States. It has a pea comb, which makes it ideal for northern climates, where regular combs can be susceptible to frostbite. It was developed in the United States from large chickens from the port of Shanghai, China, and specimens were presented as a gift to Queen Victoria, creating a sensation in England.

Standard weights: Cock: 12 lbs.; Hen: 10 lbs.

> *"Without ~~friends~~ **chickens** no one would choose to live, though he had all other goods."* —Aristotle

Chickens have the ability to sleep with one eye open. The two hemispheres of their brains are each wired to an eye and can operate independently. In unihemispheric slow-wave sleep, half their brain gets a snooze while the other side (and opposite eye) remains awake. In a row of chickens sleeping on a roost, the ones in the middle will close both eyes and sleep, while the two end chickens will leave their outermost eye open to keep watch. Partway through the night, they will rotate so the other half of their brain gets rest.

〜〜〜〜

Because of the ratio of body weight to wing area, chickens are not capable of sustained flight. Lighter birds are the best fliers. The longest recorded flight of a domestic chicken is thirteen seconds.

NUGGET OF CHICKEN WISDOM:

Even if you can't fly, you can still flap your wings.

In Japan, it has become a tradition to eat fried chicken on Christmas Eve. In a country where about 1 percent of the population counts itself as Christian, this tradition started in the early 1970s, when foreigners couldn't find turkey for their holiday meal and ate Kentucky Fried Chicken instead. The company saw a marketing opportunity, and now they sell a meal that includes cake and champagne. KFC records its highest worldwide sales day of the year on December 24. In the United States, the highest sales come on Mother's Day.

> *"It takes a tough man to make a tender chicken."* —Frank Perdue

Don't throw away your eggshells! Crush them finely and feed them to your chickens in place of the crushed oyster shells supplement that provides them with needed calcium. Other uses for ground eggshells include facials, garden pest control, and laundry whitener.

Baby chicks are known to be precocial upon hatching, or mobile and relatively mature. Chicks come out of the egg with their eyes open, covered with down, and able to feed themselves and walk on their own.

～～～～

It's official: the egg came before the chicken. All vertebrates have eggs, but reptiles were laying theirs long before the evolution of birds.

～～～～

As hens grow older, they produce larger eggs. Production, however, declines each year.

～～～～

In 1981, The Chicken Dance was introduced to the United States by a German band during the Oktoberfest in Tulsa, Oklahoma. In German, the song was actually called "the duck dance," but a duck costume could not be found. A chicken costume was located at a local TV station.

Cochin

This ancient Chinese breed of chicken came to the United States and England in the mid-nineteenth century at the end of the Opium Wars, which opened China to trade with the West. This massive, docile, feather-legged chicken was twice the size of an average English breed. Queen Victoria and her husband, Prince Albert, were enthusiasts of the birds and added them to their menagerie, where they were fed a mixture of boiled rice, potatoes, and milk. In addition to its size, the profusion of feathers makes the Cochin a stately bird. It is known to be a homebody and can be prone to becoming fat due to inactivity, which negatively affects its egg laying.

Standard weights: Cock: 11 lbs.; Hen: 8.5 lbs.

> *"The key to everything is patience. You get the chicken by hatching the egg, not by smashing it."* —Arnold H. Glasow

The crop of a chicken is a small pocket at the beginning of the digestive system and is where a chicken stores food. Then the food moves to the stomach. The gizzard comes after the stomach and is where gravel and grit eaten by the bird helps to "chew" the food.

〰〰〰

Chickens have demonstrated self-control. Given the choice between an immediate access to less food versus a delayed access to more food, chickens were able to discriminate and make the choice most beneficial to them in the long term. Humans are not able to do this until the age of four.

NUGGET OF CHICKEN WISDOM:

There are advantages to being smarter than people think you are.

Chicken Demidoff

There are two chicken dishes named after Russian prince Anatole Demidoff. One is a boned, stuffed chicken covered with a rich sauce; the other has filleted chicken sautéed in butter and topped with puréed root vegetables, then artichoke hearts and sliced onions, and finished off with a truffle slice. The sauce consists of the cooking juices, Madeira, and demi-glace. Prince Demidoff, a known gourmand, grew up in Paris, adored Napoleon, and briefly married Napoleon's niece.

〰〰

Tonic immobility is the fear-induced catatonic state a chicken can enter when a straight line is drawn on the ground in front of their beaks. The chicken will focus on the line and become hypnotized and motionless.

"America will never be destroyed from the outside. If we falter and lose our freedoms, it will be because we destroyed ~~ourselves~~ our chickens." —Abraham Lincoln

Chickens will poop
while sleeping.

~~~~

The largest chicken egg on record weighed
nearly twelve ounces. It was a five-yolk egg laid by
a black Minorca in Lancashire, England, in 1896.

~~~~

Unlike other birds, a mother hen does not feed her young
by putting food directly into their beaks. Rather, she leads
them to appropriate food and water sources and teaches
them to feed themselves. Chicks are, however, dependent
on their mother for warmth and protection for
several weeks until they are fully feathered.

~~~~

As part of some wedding ceremonies in China,
a chicken can stand in for an important guest
or family member unable to attend. A close
relative holds the chicken, which wears a
piece of red silk over its head.

Rhode Island Red

Long one of the most popular backyard chicken breeds, this dual-purpose bird is both an enthusiastic egg layer and a good meat chicken. A healthy hen can lay up to five to six eggs per week. Rhode Island Reds are known for their hardiness, friendliness, and feistiness. Developed in Little Compton, Rhode Island, in the nineteenth century, the original sire of the breed is a Malay chicken that is on display in the Smithsonian Institution.

Standard weights: Cock: 8.7 lbs.; Hen: 6.5 lbs.

> *"I've learned that people will forget what you said, people will forget what you did, but people will never forget how you made them* ~~feel~~ *some chicken."* —Maya Angelou

A special rooster call of "took, took, took" is his way of letting his hens know he has found food. But if they have food already, they will ignore him.

〰〰

Some varieties of chicken have an extra toe. Most chickens have four toes, three pointing forward and one behind. In the breeds with five toes, such as Silkies, Dorkings, and Sultans, the extra toe never touches the ground.

〰〰

It takes twenty-one days for a hen to hatch an egg. An egg needs to be kept at 86°F in order to develop into a chick.

NUGGET OF CHICKEN WISDOM:

If somebody new comes into your flock who doesn't look like you, give it a couple of days and you will forget that you haven't always known them.

A fresh egg has a cloudy white; an older egg has a clear white. Carbon dioxide, which is naturally present in fresh-laid eggs, slowly escapes through the pores of the shell over time, clearing the white.

〰〰〰

The American Egg Board is a marketing organization responsible for the slogan "The Incredible, Edible Egg." Created in 1976, it is funded by the nation's largest egg producers.

〰〰〰

The process of breaking through the eggshell is called pipping. Chicks have a "pipping muscle" on the back of their necks, which gives them the strength to break through the hard shell. When the chicks are too large to absorb oxygen through the pores of the shell, they use their egg tooth—a small, bony protuberance on the top of the end of the beak—to break into the air cell at the end of the egg, which gives them several hours of oxygen. Shortly after the chick hatches, the egg tooth falls off.

Although there are hundreds of different breeds of chicken worldwide, the American Poultry Association recognizes sixty-five at the time of writing this book. This does not include the dominant industrial breeds.

> *"All you need is love. But a little ~~chocolate~~ chicken now and then doesn't hurt."* —Charles M. Schulz

The first "Why did the chicken cross the road?" riddle appeared in print in an 1847 issue of *The Knickerbocker,* a monthly magazine in New York. The punch line was "Because it wanted to get to the other side!"

Sebright

The Sebright is a bantam chicken that was developed by Sir John Sebright, an English breeder who wanted a bantam with a laced plumage. Sebright was a selective breeder whose animal experiments influenced the work of Charles Darwin. Sebrights have a distinct carriage, with breasts thrust prominently forward, a very short back, and a tail that sticks behind like a rudder. A truly ornamental breed, they lay limited numbers of tiny, white eggs and can be difficult to raise.

Standard weights: Cock: 22 oz.; Hen: 20 oz.

The scientific name for a chicken is *Gallus gallus domesticus*, given to it by Carl Linnaeus in 1758.

> *"I did not become a vegetarian for my health, I did it for the health of the chickens."* —Isaac Bashevis Singer

The fear of chickens is called alektorophobia. Famed German film director Werner Herzog suffers from it.

〜〜〜〜

Chicken soup is more than just comfort food. The meat of a chicken contains cysteine, an amino acid that is related to the active ingredient in a drug used to treat bronchitis. In 2011, a study in Iowa determined that people with viral illnesses who ate chicken soup had faster recoveries than people who did not.

In ancient Roman times, special soothsaying cakes were sometimes given to chickens. If the chicken quietly ate the cake, one could count on good fortune ahead. If the chicken was agitated and made excessive noise or flapped its wings, it was considered an ill omen.

"The difference between involvement and commitment is like ham and eggs. The chicken is involved; the pig is committed."
—Martina Navratilova

Chickens start to communicate a day or so before they are hatched. A mother hen has a purring sound to talk to her young when they are still in the shell, and the chicks begin to peep back at her from within the egg.

NUGGET OF CHICKEN WISDOM:

Communicate continuously: chickens never stop talking to each other. They mutter and cluck and squawk and complain, even when they're roosting.

Egg candling is the practice of shining a light into a fertilized egg to determine the viability of the potential chick inside. The name comes from the fact that it used to be done with a candle and now can be done with a flashlight or with commercially made egg candlers.

〰〰〰

Chickens signal when they are ready to lay. Before she lays an egg, the comb of a hen will get redder and larger.

〰〰〰

Bantam chickens are one-third to one-half the size of standard chickens. Some are true bantams with no larger counterpart, and some are miniaturized versions. The roosters are known to be puffed up and aggressive. The name comes from the port city of Bantam in Indonesia, where ships would stock up on chickens for their journeys. The small chickens were useful on board, producing eggs while taking up little space.

Leghorn

The Leghorn is a breed of chicken whose name is an anglicized form of "Livorno," the part of Italy where it originates. After they were introduced to the United States, they were known as "Italian chickens." The most common form of Leghorn is the white variety, which is a good layer of large, white eggs, with yearly egg production reaching over three hundred (other varieties not being as prolific). The white Leghorn produces most of the white eggs sold in American grocery stores. The Leghorn's temperament is described as active, intelligent, and even ambitious.

Standard weights: Cock: 6 lbs.; Hen: 5.1 lbs.

> *"If you tell the ~~truth~~ chickens, you don't have to remember anything."* —Mark Twain

Chickens have a third eyelid, the nictitating eyelid. Used for protection, it moves from front to back rather than up or down and keeps dust, dirt, and other debris out of their eyes.

Chickens are the closest living relative to Tyrannosaurus rex. When a rare T. rex fossil was found, scientists analyzed the proteins and found they more closely resembled bird proteins, particularly ostriches and chickens, than other reptiles.

Chickens model their behavior on each other. For instance, a broody hen can encourage other hens in the flock to become broody as well.

NUGGET OF
CHICKEN
WISDOM:

Pay no attention to complainers;
they are usually just talking to
themselves.

Foghorn Leghorn is a fictional Southern good ol' boy white Leghorn rooster featured in twenty-eight different Looney Tunes cartoons and voiced by the legendary Mel Blanc. The persona was based on another fictional character, Senator Beauregard Claghorn, who appeared on a radio show in the 1940s.

> *"If you've broken the eggs, you should make the omelet."* —Anthony Eden

Over the past one hundred or so years, commercial egg production per hen has more than tripled. In 1900, a single layer hen's average egg production was eighty-three eggs per year. One hundred years later, it is around three hundred. Selective breeding accounts for much of the increase, along with diet and artificial lighting to manipulate the egg-laying cycle.

NASA is testing a jet fuel made from chicken fat. It's called hydrotreated renewable jet fuel. The U.S. military has a goal of eventually flying aircraft using 50 percent biofuel.

~~~~

The chicken's genome was sequenced in 2004. Chickens have between 20,000 and 23,000 genes, and only 1 billion DNA base pairs, as compared with our 2.9 billion pairs.

~~~~

Chicken à la King
Diced chicken with mushrooms and peppers or other vegetables in a sherry cream sauce. There are a handful of conflicting origin stories, but the *New York Times* credited the dish to William "Bill" King, a cook in the late 1800s who worked at the Bellevue Hotel in Philadelphia. Usually served over noodles, rice, or toast.

Naked Neck

Originally from Transylvania, Romania, the Naked Neck chicken is more common in Europe and South America than in North America. It has a small patch of feathers under the full comb on top of its head and then features bare skin down to the shoulders. This breed is sometimes called the Turken, because of the mistaken notion that it is a hybrid between a chicken and a domestic turkey. The trait for "nakedness" gives it a number of characteristics that are considered desirable. It has half the number of feathers of a normal chicken and can tolerate higher heat; and because of its low feather count, it is easier to pluck.

Standard weights: Cock: 8.5 lbs.; Hen: 6.5 lbs.

"Think where man's glory most begins and ends, and say my glory was I had such ~~friends~~ chickens."
—William Butler Yeats

In 1948, the Great Atlantic & Pacific Tea Company, otherwise known as the A&P, sponsored a nationwide chicken competition to select the breed of chicken that would be called the Chicken of Tomorrow. The company wanted a breed of chicken that would be raised expressly for meat. There were two winners, whose genetics were crossed to make the fast-growing Cornish Cross, which now dominates the commercial broiler chicken industry.

〰〰〰〰

Established in 1873, the American Poultry Association is the oldest poultry organization in the United States and is actually the oldest livestock association in North America.

In most cases, hens with white earlobes will lay white eggs and hens with red earlobes will lay brown eggs.

〰〰〰〰

Egg size and grade are not the same. Size is determined by weight per dozen. Grade refers to the quality of the shell, white, and yolk and the size of the air cell.

〰〰〰〰

Chicken pox has nothing to do with chickens. English is the only language in which the disease is connected to the chicken. Other countries name it after the Varicellovirus that causes it. Numerous theories exist for the name "chicken pox"—that it was thought to be a milder form of smallpox, therefore it was a "chicken" virus, or that the blisters look like a chicken pecked the victim.

〰〰〰〰

Poultry manure has long been used as a fertilizer, and in its carbonized form, the manure is now being studied as part of a wastewater treatment program that can absorb pollutants in water.

"What of the hens whom we observe each day at home, with what care and assiduity they govern and guard their chicks? Some let down their wings for the chicks to come under; others arch their backs for them to climb upon; there is no part of their bodies with which they do not wish to cherish their chicks if they can, nor do they do this without a joy and alacrity which they seem to exhibit by the sound of their voices." —Plutarch

A chicken's beak is highly sensitive. The beak is alive—with numerous nerve endings, it is used to explore, detect, and defend. What makes the beak such a sensitive part of the chicken is something called the bill tip organ, which allows chickens to discriminate between what is food and what is not.

〰〰

Mother hens teach their baby chicks what is good for them to eat and what is bad. In tests, baby chicks learned from their mothers to stay away from certain color-coded grains that are bad for them.

NUGGET OF CHICKEN WISDOM:

The young watch everything you do. Pay mind to what you do in front of them.

Silkie

An ornamental bantam (miniature) chicken known for its fluffy, silklike plumage, its black meat and bones, and its docile temperament. An ancient breed originating in China, it came to Europe via the Silk Road. Marco Polo wrote of it as a "furry chicken," and in the West it was billed as being the offspring of a chicken and a rabbit. The silkies' feathers lack barbicels, the tiny barbs that hook the filaments of a feather together into a sheath. Because of this, the Silkie is unable to fly. Silkie hens are known to be broody and don't like to leave the nest and so can be used to incubate and raise the young of other species.

Standard weights: Cock: 4 lbs.; Hen: 3 lbs.

> *"When I started counting my* ~~blessings~~ ***chickens**, my whole life turned around."* —Willie Nelson

The Maillard reaction is what gives cooked chicken its flavor and why roasted chicken generally tastes better, for instance, than boiled chicken. Named after French chemist Louis Camille Maillard, who discovered the process in 1912, it is the chemical reaction between amino acids in protein molecules and simple sugars that happens when the temperature rises to between 300°F and 500°F.

〰〰〰

Chickens have finely tuned senses, being able to hear low and high frequencies, and simultaneously see long-range and close-up. And, like most birds, they can orient to magnetic fields.

〰〰〰

Tidbitting is a rooster dance in which they make their food calls and move their head up and down, picking up and dropping a tidbit of food. Females prefer males that tidbit well and that have large, vibrant combs.

NUGGET OF
CHICKEN
WISDOM:

Everybody loves a rooster that
knows how to dance.

Chicken Maria Theresia

A luxurious dish of poached chicken breasts and sliced beef tongue in a cream sauce. Named for the queen of Hungary and Bohemia.

"I want there to be no peasant in my kingdom so poor that he cannot have a chicken in his pot every Sunday."
—King Henry IV

A chef's hat or toque, is said to have a pleat for each of the many ways you can cook an egg.

The world's largest omelet was made with 145,000 eggs, weighed over 14,000 pounds, and required a frying pan 34 feet across. This feat was accomplished in 2012 in Portugal.

The average natural life span of a chicken is highly dependent on environment and breeding and is therefore hard to gauge. Most people think it is about eight to ten years, with pure breeds having greater odds for a long life than hybrid breeds. A chicken named Matilda was the first to be awarded the title of World's Oldest Living Chicken from Guinness World Records. She lived an additional two years after capturing the title and died at age sixteen. She was a nonlaying hen and worked as a magician's assistant for her owners in Bessemer, Alabama. Matilda's record held for just a few years. In 2009, an Australian chicken named Blacky took over the title.

〰〰〰

Civilizations in Southeast Asia were the first to domesticate the chicken, starting at least five thousand years ago. The red junglefowl was captured and bred, not for food but for fighting. Due to interbreeding with domestic chickens, the wild red junglefowl faces a threat of extinction.

BREED SPOTLIGHT

Ayam Cemani

An Indonesian chicken recently introduced to the rest of the world from Java, the Ayam Cemani is black inside and out. Dubbed as the Lamborghini of poultry, its comb, claws, beak, organs, and meat are black. This excess pigmentation is caused by a genetic condition known as fibromelanosis. These chickens were used in spiritual ceremonies in Java, as their blackness was seen as a bridge to the spirit world. Although they are friendly birds, the hens are inattentive parents, laying pale-pink eggs that other hens then need to hatch and raise. Appropriately, there is a black market for the Ayam Cemani, with individual chickens netting in the thousands of dollars.

Standard weights: Cock: 6.5 lbs.; Hen: 4.5 lbs.

> *"A hen is only an egg's way of making another egg."* —Samuel Butler

There are more chickens in the world than there are any other bird species. Chickens number around 25 billion, which means chickens outnumber people more than three to one. The bird in distant second place is the common pheasant, which numbers around 173 million.

Chickens love dust baths. They will dig a shallow pit in the dirt, spread their wings, and use their feet to kick dust up into their feathers. This helps chickens maintain proper feather insulation and also wards off mites and other parasites.

In the Middle Ages, chicken soup was used as an aphrodisiac, particularly in the spring, with fresh garlic and available greens.

NUGGET OF CHICKEN WISDOM:

Don't be afraid of a little dirt.

There are four locales in the United States with "chicken" in their names: Chicken, Alaska (pop: 7); Chicken Bristle, in both Illinois and Kentucky, named after cockfighting; and Chickentown, Pennsylvania, officially designated not as a town but as a populated area.

> *"It is not a lack of love, but a lack of ~~friendship~~ **chickens** that makes unhappy marriages."* —Friedrich Nietzsche

Eggs contain about the highest-quality food protein known. It is second only to mother's milk for human nutrition.

Kung Pao Chicken

Popular on Chinese restaurant menus in the United States, kung pao chicken is a dish of small pieces of stir-fried chicken with peppers and peanuts. The dish was named for Ding Baozhen, governor of Sichuan in the late 1800s. His official title was gong bao, from which "kung pao" derived.

〰〰〰

Female chickens are pullets until they're old enough to lay eggs and become hens.

〰〰〰

An eggshell has seventeen thousand pores on its surface and so is permeable to air and moisture. Placing a truffle alongside fresh eggs in storage will impart a bit of truffle flavor to the eggs.

Marans

The Marans is a breed of chicken descended from Asian stock that was left behind by seafarers in the port town of Marans, France. Originally bred as fighting cocks, they were domesticated by the early 1800s. Recognized varieties include black copper, blue birchen, golden cuckoo, and white. In addition to the deep-chocolate color of their shells, Marans chickens lay eggs that are considered the best tasting in the world, with a firm yolk that features excellent "muscle tone." British author Ian Fleming identified Marans eggs as those preferred by James Bond.

Standard weights: Cock: 8.5 lbs.; Hen: 7 lbs.

> *"The longer I live, the more beautiful ~~life~~ a chicken becomes."*
> —Frank Lloyd Wright

A chicken's right eye is nearsighted, which is good for finding food at close range, and a chicken's left eye is farsighted, which helps it monitor for predators or other threats, especially ones in the sky. You'll almost always see a chicken cocking its head to the right to scan the sky with its left eye. However, some experts say that this is more due to having two foveae in their eyes (humans have one), rather than nearsightedness and farsightedness.

〜〜〜〜

Chickens are very social. The pecking order increases the odds of survival for the whole flock, strengthening the dominant birds and eliminating the weakest. Adding or taking away a member of a flock stresses all the birds. Fights will break out until a new pecking order is established.

Chickens become more docile at night. Even the feistiest chicken goes into a passive state after dusk, so the best time to handle or move a chicken is at night.

〰〰〰

Chickens do not produce urine. Through their high respiration rate, chickens lose most excess moisture through breathing. The white part of a chicken dropping is the uric acid.

"And so, my fellow Americans: ask not what your ~~country~~ chicken can do for you—ask what you can do for your ~~country~~ chicken."
—John F. Kennedy

Deep frying chicken in fat was originally a Scottish tradition. Scottish immigrants to America introduced the practice to African slaves in the American South.

NUGGET OF CHICKEN WISDOM:

Just because you're part
of a pecking order
doesn't mean you
have to peck.

Chicken feathers can be used in the manufacture of paper products, for air filters, wallboard, or decorative wallpaper.

A castrated rooster is called a capon. After castration, the wattles and comb stop growing, which can make the capon appear to have a small head. Capon meat is known for being more tender, fatty, and flavorful than regular chicken.

The egg-laying process of a hen begins in her eye, sort of. The light cue from natural sunlight or artificial light stimulates a photoreceptor gland near the eye, which in turn triggers the release of an egg cell from the chicken's ovary. The pineal gland is so close to the chicken's relatively thin skull that even a blind chicken can sense enough light via the pineal gland to start the process.

Yokohama

The Yokohama chicken is a showy, long-tailed breed developed in Germany in part from the Japanese long-tailed Minohiki breed. Yokohama plumage is either pure white or white with red saddle feathers; their tails can be three to four feet long. Yokohamas have a very alert temperament and are happiest when they are free to wander a large distance. They lay only seventy-eight to one hundred small eggs annually and become broody after about twelve to fourteen eggs. Chicks require extra protein as they grow their tails.

Standard weights: Cock: 5.5 lbs.; Hen: 4 lbs.

> "Big nations are like chickens. They like to make big noises, but very often it is no more than squabbling." —Albert Schweitzer

Double-yolk eggs occur in about one in a thousand eggs. Double yolks happen when two yolks are released from the ovary so close together that one shell forms around the both of them. They occur mostly to new layers struggling with shifting hormones that affect yolk release from the ovary, and occasionally to older hens at the end of their egg production.

Le *poulet de Bresse* is a legendarily tasty bird from France, in fact said to be the best-tasting chicken. The influential French gastronome Jean Anthelme Brillat-Savarin declared the Bresse chicken to be "the queen of poultry, and the poultry of kings." Its production is highly regulated: any chicken sold as a Bresse must be raised within a legally defined area of the region of Bresse in east-central France. Its diet is likewise highly controlled. The birds are kept free range for four months, with a diet low in protein so they will forage for insects. Either in the market or in the high-end restaurants of Paris, Bresse chicken commands premium prices. Only 10 percent are allowed for export.

Calcium in a hen's diet is necessary for the production of strong eggshells. Calcium is easily found in ground oyster shells, among other sources. If hens don't get enough calcium in their diet, they will solve the problem themselves by eating their own eggs, which once begun is a hard habit to stop. Faded color in the wattles and comb is a sign of calcium deficiency.

~~~~

Chickens molt each fall. As light diminishes, new feathers push out old ones. Egg production drops along with the feathers. To keep the chickens in optimal health during molting, extra protein in the form of mealworms or black sunflower seeds may be added to the diet.

"I met a lot of hard-boiled eggs in my life, but you, you're twenty minutes."
—Billy Wilder, *Ace in the Hole* (1951)

Eggs are placed in cartons with the small end up in order to keep the air cell in place and the yolk centered.

NUGGET OF CHICKEN WISDOM:

Take good care of your feathers.

Chicken Picasso

Named after the Spanish painter Pablo Picasso and said to have been created by him. It is a casserole dish made of chicken breasts cooked with bell peppers and plenty of onions and spices, topped with a generous amount of cheese. In northern Italy, a version of it features tomatoes and basil pesto.

In 2006/2007, very old Polynesian chicken bones were discovered on a dig on the coast of Chile—bones so old that they call into doubt Christopher Columbus being the first outsider to "discover" America. The bones may indicate that Polynesians landed on South America's west coast and explored inland, possibly as much as a century prior to Columbus.

As anyone who has tried to capture a chicken knows, they can have startling bursts of speed. Chickens can run up to 9 mph.

BREED SPOTLIGHT
Hamburg

This small but showy chicken originated in Holland prior to the fourteenth century. It is said that the first chicken show ever was conducted in a pub in England in 1800 and started over whose Hamburg rooster was the "most magnificent." The bartender judged, and the prize was a copper pot. Hamburgs are lively birds but intolerant of confinement and prefer to roost in dense, tall hedges or high in trees, contributing to the once-popular belief that Hamburgs were a hybrid of common chicken and wild pheasant. L. Frank Baum, the creator of the Wizard of Oz stories, was a Hamburg chicken enthusiast. His first book before the Oz series was a treatise on the raising of the different varieties of Hamburgs.

Standard weights: Cock: 5 lbs.; Hen: 4 lbs.

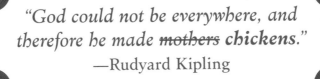

"God could not be everywhere, and therefore he made ~~mothers~~ chickens."
—Rudyard Kipling

Chickens experience rapid eye movement, or REM, sleep—which means they are capable of dreaming. However, their REM sleep lasts for seconds, while ours can go for minutes to an hour.

September is National Chicken Month. That month was chosen by the National Chicken Council for a special emphasis on marketing because of declining chicken sales when people turn off their barbecues for the season.

Fleshy combs and wattles are a chicken's means to cool itself. Blood circulates through both, cooling the bird. For the same reason, combs and wattles expose a chicken to the cold, with large combs being vulnerable to frostbite and small combs distinguishing the most cold-hardy breeds.

〰〰〰〰

Mature male chickens less than one year old are called cockerels. Cockerels usually start crowing before four months old.

"God helps them that help ~~themselves~~ chickens."
—Benjamin Franklin

NUGGET OF
CHICKEN
WISDOM:

A good cackle can reset your
whole day.

Some farmers add small amounts of dried, crushed marigold petals to chicken feed in order to make the yolks of their eggs a darker yellow.

~~~~

Chickens have as many as thirty different vocalizations, to communicate with each other about food, danger, distress, and aggression.

~~~~

Older eggs float in water, while fresher ones sink. A hard-boiled egg will spin; an uncooked one will wobble.

~~~~

Chicken feet are used in voodoo as charms for a powerful form of protection against theft of any kind, whether of love or possessions. The most powerful chicken's feet are thought to come from chickens with black feathers.

Barnevelder

The rare Barnevelder chicken originated in Holland more than 200 years ago, and was bred from crossing local chickens with birds coming into Europe from Asia. This handsome chicken has a double lace pattern on each feather (found primarily in females) and lays dark chocolate-colored eggs. The bird has an easygoing temperament, to the extent that even Barnevelder roosters are known to nurture baby chicks.

Standard weights: Cock: 7 lbs.; Hen: 6 lbs.

> *"Business is never so healthy as when, like a chicken, it must do a certain amount of scratching for what it gets."* —Henry Ford

Chickens prefer to roost in the same spot at night.

~~~~

The American Standard of Perfection is the American Poultry Association's official breed standard reference by which all show chickens are judged. Its symbol is a wishbone and feather.

~~~~

It typically takes a hen between twenty-five and twenty-seven hours to produce an egg, which can make them lay slightly later every day than the day before. However, some hens can lay multiple eggs in a day. The most eggs laid by a single hen recorded in one day is seven.

NUGGET OF CHICKEN WISDOM:

If you sit on anything long enough,
it might hatch.

Chicken is the tenth sign in the twelve signs in the Chinese zodiac. Those born under the sign of the rooster are ascribed loyalty and keen powers of observation. The next Year of the Rooster will be 2029.

"But my favorite remained the basic roast chicken. What a deceptively simple dish. I had come to believe that one can judge the quality of a cook by his or her roast chicken. Above all, it should taste like chicken: it should be so good that even a perfectly simple, buttery roast should be a delight."
—Julia Child, *My Life in France*

Big Bird is the eight-foot two-inch avian character on *Sesame Street* played since 1969 by Caroll Spinney. Big Bird can sing, ice skate, roller skate, dance, swim, sing (although not well), write poetry, and ride a unicycle, and is assumed by most to be a chicken. Big Bird is not a chicken. He is a canary.

Chicken egg color does not affect the nutrition of the egg. The nutrition of the egg comes from the diet of the chicken.

〜〜〜〜

The rooster crowing sound is typically spelled out as "cock-a-doodle-doo" in American English.

In French, it's *cocorico*.

In German, it's *kickeriki*.

In Spanish, it's *quiquiriquí,* and in Catalan and Basque it's *kikkirikí*.

In Cantonese, it's *gokogoko*. In Mandarin, it's *gou gou*.

In Dutch, it's *kukeleku*.

In Gaelic, it's *cuc-a-dudal-du*.

In Hindi, it's *kukruukuu*.

In Italian, it's *chicchirichí*.

In Icelandic, it's *gaggala gaggala gú*.

In Thai, it's *ake-e-ake-ake*.

Araucana

The Araucana is a rare breed of chicken. It has a number of characteristics that make it both unusual and difficult to breed. It is one of the only chickens to lay an egg that is blue on both the inside and outside of the shell (as opposed to brown eggs, which are brown only on the outside). The Araucana is a great flier but lacks tail feathers. It also sports tufts of feathers on either side of its head, but the gene for that tuft is lethal to 20 percent of the chicks. It is not known whether the bird derives from chickens brought by Europeans after 1492 or if it was already present in South America.

Standard weights: Cock: 6 lbs.; Hen: 5 lbs.

> *"If you're going through hell, keep ~~going~~ chickens."* —Winston Churchill

Chickens have more bones in their necks than humans, or giraffes. All mammals have exactly seven vertebrae in their necks; birds have anywhere from thirteen to twenty-five, giving their necks flexibility needed to preen, find food, maintain balance, and absorb shocks.

〰〰〰

Chicken personality is related to place in the pecking order. Even as breeds exhibit personality traits, the top chicken within a flock tends to be louder and feistier, while bottom chickens tend to be more shy and watchful. The habit of feather pecking, however, is more related to stress due to such things as not enough space in the coop.

NUGGET OF CHICKEN WISDOM:

Flashier roosters tend to have lots of hens.

Multiple roosters can get along in a flock, provided there are enough hens for each. Most experts recommend a minimum of eight to ten hens per rooster, but some breeds may do well enough with a minimum of three to four hens per rooster.

Chicken consumption is expected to increase by 24 percent over the next ten years, replacing pork, which is currently number one. By 2025, chicken will account for 50 percent of the world's meat consumption. The world's top exporter of chicken is the Netherlands, while China breeds the most chickens: 4.5 billion annually.

"If you judge ~~people~~ chickens, you have no time to love them." —Mother Teresa

Chickens roost close together during the night for warmth, stability, and protection, but they'll usually start spreading out more in the hours before daybreak.

A common superstition in the American South is that one must never eat chicken on the first day of the new year. Because chickens scratch for food, the belief is that one who eats chicken on New Year's Day will have to "scratch" to find sustenance all year long.

Kapparah is a ritual atonement practiced by some on the eve of Yom Kippur, or the Day of Atonement, one of the Jewish holy days. A chicken is waved or swung over the head and is then given to charity, either live or butchered in accordance with halachic rules. Some Orthodox communities are instead advocating hugging a chicken, rather than swinging it overhead, to release the person's sins into the bird.

In 1943, under wartime rationing, adult British subjects were allowed one fresh egg per week.

BREED SPOTLIGHT

Sumatra

The Sumatra chicken is native to the island of Sumatra in Indonesia and was originally imported to the West for the purpose of cockfighting. Today, the Sumatra is kept mainly for its beauty, with abundant flowing feathers and lustrous plumage. Unlike most modern chickens, Sumatras are strong fliers and were said to sometimes fly between the islands of Sumatra, Java, and Borneo. Sumatras breed seasonally, becoming fertile only in the spring. Although prized for their ornamental qualities, Sumatras are on the watch list by The Livestock Conservancy.

Standard weights: Cock: 6 lbs.; Hen: 4 lbs.

> *"The chicken does not exist only in order to produce another egg. He may also exist to amuse himself, to praise God, and even to suggest ideas to a French dramatist."*
> —G. K. Chesterton, *What's Wrong With the World*

The first American poultry show was held November 15, 1849, at the Boston Public Garden. The person behind the show was Dr. John Bennett of Plymouth, Massachusetts, who boasted of having the best and best-looking fowl, and he "respectfully invited" other breeders to bring their best to compare. More than ten thousand visitors came to see the hundreds of exhibitors. The show turned enough of a profit to ensure its annual return.

〜〜〜〜

Eggs from pasture-raised chickens have twice as much vitamin D and A, more beta-carotene, and less cholesterol and fatty acids than eggs from cage-raised birds.

NUGGET OF CHICKEN WISDOM:

Enough space to flap one's wings and explore brings out the best in one's character.

The Zoroastrian religion in ancient Persia considered the chicken a sacred animal, as roosters crowed before dawn, waking up the world and chasing away the darkness.

〜〜〜〜

Chicken feathers are made out of a strong protein called keratin. Chicken feathers can be made into strong plastic composites for car dashboards and boat exteriors. A further benefit is that, unlike petroleum-based plastics, chicken feathers will biodegrade.

> *"So many* ~~books~~ *chickens, so little time."* —Frank Zappa

Eugene, Oregon, is the American city most compatible with urban backyard chicken raising, boasting the most gardens, greenhouses, and chicken coops per capita. According to the U.S. Department of Agriculture, 15 percent of the world's food is grown in urban areas.

General Tso's Chicken

A staple at American Chinese restaurants, General Tso's chicken consists of fried chicken pieces in a sweet, slightly spicy sauce, usually served with broccoli. The actual General Tso was a Qing dynasty statesman and military leader, but the connection to the dish is unclear. At the U.S. Naval Academy, the same dish is called Admiral Tso's chicken.

〰〰

Chickens have a 300-degree range of vision without moving their heads. In comparison, humans' range of vision is 180 degrees.

〰〰

Although they do not like to, chickens can swim. When floating in the water, they paddle their feet like a duck to shore. However, they cannot last too long in water, as their feathers can become waterlogged, even in the rain.

For Cluck's Sake! copyright © 2018 by Stacia Tolman. All rights reserved. Printed in China.
No part of this book may be used or reproduced in any manner whatsoever
without written permission except in the case of reprints in the context of reviews.

Andrews McMeel Publishing
a division of Andrews McMeel Universal
1130 Walnut Street, Kansas City, Missouri 64106

www.andrewsmcmeel.com

18 19 20 21 22 SHO 10 9 8 7 6 5 4 3 2 1

ISBN: 978-1-4494-9451-3

Library of Congress Control Number: 2018930818

Page 33 iStock.com/trendmakers, page 81 iStock.com/lepas2004,
page 93 iStock.com/andrewburgess

The rest of the images used under license from Shutterstock.com

Editor: Melissa Rhodes
Acquiring Editor: Marti Petty
Art Director/Designer: Julie Barnes
Production Editor: Elizabeth A. Garcia
Production Manager: Tamara Haus

ATTENTION: SCHOOLS AND BUSINESSES
Andrews McMeel books are available at quantity discounts with bulk
purchase for educational, business, or sales promotional use. For information,
please e-mail the Andrews McMeel Publishing Special Sales Department:
specialsales@amuniversal.com.